Looking at My Grandmother's Old Letters

Dewayne Hotchkins

Rosen REAL READERS

I0809747

Rosen Classroom™
New York

My grandmother shows me letters. They are from my grandfather.

My grandfather was in the Army. He fought in the Vietnam War.

He wrote about his friends.

They helped him.

He wrote about tanks.

He wrote about fighter planes.

I learn a lot about history from the letters my grandfather wrote to my grandmother.

Words to Know

fighter plane

letter

tank

war